FLORIDA GIRL

FLORIDA
GIRL *Confessions of a Beachcomber*

To: Arthur & Denise

Good friends, good neighbors,
and fellow gardeners/artists and
photographers - lots of talents! You have
blessed my life and I wish you every
happiness in your marriage -
The Lord bless you both!
Mary Grable Renshaw

MARY GRABLE RENSHAW

MOUNTAIN ARBOR
PRESS

MOUNTAIN ARBOR
PRESS
Alpharetta, GA

ISBN: 978-1-6653-0052-0 - Paperback

Printed in the United States of America   0 1 0 8 2 1

All original artwork by Mary Grable Renshaw unless otherwise noted.

Book cover illustration and page 35 by Alice J. Walker
Guest artist Frederica Newsome, watercolor, page 63
Author photograph by Arthur Ratliff

⊗ This paper meets the requirements of ANSI/NISO Z39.48-1992 (Permanence of Paper)

FLORIDA GIRL

is dedicated

to my parents,

Warner and Dorothy Grable.

They gave me

beautiful memories to cherish forever.

ACKNOWLEDGMENTS

I am grateful to family and friends who took the time to read my poems and prose, generously offer feedback, and encourage me to put them into print. My stepdaughter, Suzannah Harris, volunteered to do the first round of editing. Suzannah has taught creative writing in a college and has a way with words, just like her father. Then editor Mary Marvella Barfield added her editorial expertise. When working with an editor, your own writing skills automatically improve. Friends Claire Hertzler, Sharon Bailey, Judy Holzman, and Judy Cox contributed valuable suggestions. Pastor Gloria Gainor of the Lighthouse Evangelistic Church in Cartersville, Georgia, was a valued source of encouragement and wisdom. Kathleen and Jim Santor were additional great sources of encouragement.

I am most grateful to God, who bestowed upon me a deep love for His creation. Once He touched my heart to see His handwriting inscribed over all the earth, it was easy to put that love into words.

There is beauty to be found everywhere, especially in my home state of Florida.

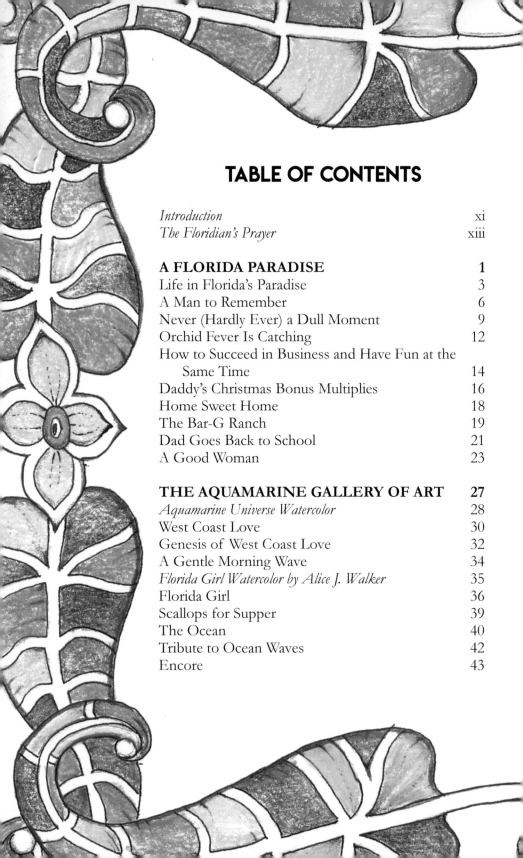

TABLE OF CONTENTS

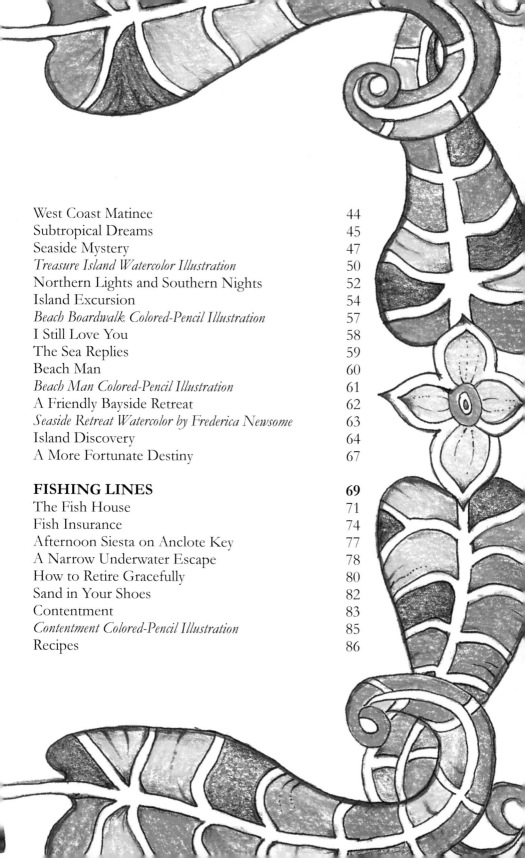

INTRODUCTION

Memories of the early years I lived in Florida are filled with so many images of its natural beauty, the exploration of beaches and bays, and of my parents' loving kindnesses to me that, eventually, I had to give them a voice. Far from the crowded tourist meccas and gift shops that offer visitors only a taste of the state's pleasures, I came to know in depth the real Florida and fell in love with it.

Visits to the nearby beaches of Florida's west coast gave us great joy. The many hours I spent swimming in the warm waters of the Gulf of Mexico, first with the help of water wings and inner tubes, made me as comfortable in the water as the fish in the sea. I acquired an extensive shell collection and learned all of their names. A large collection of sharks' teeth added to my seaside trophies. Finding driftwood was easy if you knew where to look for it, and we did. Through these visits, I acquired a lifelong love for the sea and its many gifts.

I left my beloved home state in my midtwenties to explore other pathways, but visions of deeply colored tropical foliage and flowers followed me everywhere I went. When they finally caught up with me, I picked up brush and pen to acknowledge their impressions. My love for the coastlands of Florida has endured for a lifetime, and this, too, needed expression. Life with my delightful parents gave me additional joys to include. Those quiet, peaceful, and happy years were so good that, whenever I visit these stored memories, it is like opening a treasure chest. This book comes from a deep well of cherished remembrances.

Come along with me on a journey to Florida's west coast through poems, prose, and original art to experience its natural beauty in an era gone by, before condos and high-rise hotels appeared. Breathe in the fragrance of orange blossoms and wild orchids. Listen to the music of a mockingbird, the rustle of palm fronds in the breeze, and the peaceful rhythmic sound of waves kissing the shore. Delight in lush tropical foliage and cool gulf breezes.

Explore subtropical islands only accessible by boat. Find a secret fishing hole in the Gulf of Mexico where the fish are always biting. Discover the best remote island for collecting shells. Wiggle your toes in the wet sand and let the tiny coquina mussels tickle your feet as they try to burrow between your toes.

Come walk barefoot with me through these pages, and I will introduce you to *my* Florida, a masterpiece of God's creation.

Don't forget to bring along your flip-flops for formal occasions!

THE FLORIDIAN'S PRAYER

The Lord is my Lighthouse.
I can weather any storm.
He leads me beside the Gulf Stream waters
To a carpet of sparkling white sand.
There I lie down and rest.
As I listen to the steady rhythm of the waves,
My joy returns, my peace is restored.

He fills my hands with seashells
And my heart with the wonder of His creation.
I hear the rustle of palm fronds in the breeze
And in the night, the song of the mockingbird.
These Florida sounds bring joy to my heart.

He prepares a place for me
In the midst of family and friends.
Happy memories of the past are everywhere.
Although I may walk through a valley of showers,
Still the sun shines and rainbows abound.

The fragrance of orchids and orange blossoms
Will follow me all the days of my life.
With the Lord as my Hope, my Anchor,
I can be content anywhere,
But my heart knows its greatest joy
In the Land of Flowers.
F L O R I D A

A Florida Paradise

LIFE IN FLORIDA'S PARADISE

y family home was a comfortable two-story bungalow in Tampa's Palma Ceia, a subdivision located on the Interbay Peninsula between downtown Tampa and St. Petersburg. Surrounded by the waters of Tampa Bay and close to the nearby gulf beaches, we enjoyed pleasant weather all year long. Subtropical trees, plants, and flowers thrived in our area, and on our acre of land, we had a diverse orchard.

Citrus trees on our property provided us with oranges, pink grapefruit, calamondin, and key limes. My favorite oranges were the Hamlin variety, sweet and juicy, and each year our trees were loaded. For a quick refreshing drink, we walked to the backyard, cut a small hole in the top of an orange, squeezed it, and sipped the juice. The grapefruit hung in clusters and I often marveled at the strength of the small limbs that could support four or five heavy grapefruit. A favorite breakfast treat for us was a broiled grapefruit half with the addition of honey or maple syrup and cinnamon.

Our avocado pear tree produced so much fruit that we had more than enough for ourselves, our friends, and relatives. Even our dog,

Leo, was not left out of the feast. When the ripest avocadoes fell to the ground, our cocker spaniel made a meal of them. We frequently spotted him with a fallen pear between his paws, enjoying himself. We also grew mangos, papayas, loquats, and pineapple. The papayas grew to be so large and heavy that when one fell off the tree in the middle of the night, it made such a loud noise, it would wake me up with a start!

Many of our neighbors had an orange tree or two, but we were especially blessed. My father traveled to Miami several times to obtain from its county extension service the very best varieties of fruit trees and tropical plants. He gave each one the best of care, and we reaped the harvest. Dad participated in the Mango Forum each year and joined a group of men who experimented with preparing food from native plants. He made life interesting for himself and for everyone who knew him.

Our home often served as the scene of many outdoor meals with our large family. We grilled hamburger patties and roasted ears of corn to perfection on our outdoor brick fireplace. We brought home washtubs heavy with freshly caught scallops after a morning of gathering them from a nearby bay. In our backyard, we opened the shells and removed the small hinge mussels, which my mother then would prepare for the feast that followed. Neighbors often shared their latest catch of fresh fish with us. One of our friends, who lived at nearby Indian Rocks Beach, occasionally surprised us with stone crab claws from his traps in the Gulf. An occasional treat of smoked mullet purchased from a causeway restaurant made for a pleasant change. We lived happily in this wonderful "Garden of Eating."

We also enjoyed the Spanish and Cuban cuisine for which the Tampa area is known. Once a month, our family visited a Spanish restaurant in Ybor City, usually accompanied by friends. One of our favorite dishes was Spanish bean soup served with crisp Cuban bread. The major ingredients were garbanzo beans (chickpeas) and potatoes flavored with saffron. We loved the collard green soup, chicken with yellow rice (*arroz con pollo*), filet steak served with *catalana* sauce (my favorite), *picadillo* (a type of Spanish beef hash), and *boliche* (roast beef Spanish style). For dessert, there was Spanish caramel custard (*flan de leche acaramelado*) and coconut ice cream. We topped our meal with a cup of Cuban coffee for those who liked their coffee strong.

Life was good to us in our Florida Paradise.

A MAN TO REMEMBER

y father had an irrepressible sense of humor. I learned that when he was a teenager he got into his share of mischief. Nothing serious, mainly such things as stealing oranges from nearby orange groves, going for joy rides in the cars of neighbors, and raiding the porch ice boxes of perfect strangers. He soon realized that his friends were more serious about their mischief than he was. At the same time, a close friend invited him to a Youth for Christ rally where he made a commitment of his life to Jesus Christ. God then took this mischievous, fun-loving bent of his and turned it to the good, and my father became the most beloved person in our entire family. Wherever he was he had people laughing. His joy was contagious. He could make me laugh so hard that tears would roll down my cheeks. I miss that.

Dad loved to introduce his major interests to others. A member of the Audubon Society, he gave to a number of friends the Roger Tory Peterson book *A Field Guide to the Birds*. His own personal copy was well marked with notations of the various birds he had identified. We avoided the use of harmful chemicals in our garden because of the effect it would have upon the birds. One day, I received an unforgettable lesson. When I saw an army of grasshoppers munching on our azalea bushes, I took quick action, grabbed a box of Seven Dust, and began liberally spreading it over the poor grasshoppers. When Dad caught me in action, he informed me that poisoned grasshoppers could kill or sicken any bird that eats them. I was given a hose to wash off the poison dust. Lesson learned.

When a neighbor's cat began to trespass upon our bird sanctuary, Dad decided to discourage the cat's poaching activities. The next time the cat showed up, Dad picked up his BB gun, waited for the cat to turn its back, and fired away. The cat jumped four feet in the air and took off running. Dad, a compassionate man, examined the animal for possible wounds at the next opportunity. There were none. He hadn't intended to hurt the cat—only discourage its visits. Thereafter, all that was necessary was for him to use his "Have-a-Heart Gun." He would open the sliding glass doors of our Florida room and clap his hands loudly. The results were similar. The cat would jump high in the air and disappear. Our bird population returned to its peaceful existence, and my father was well pleased with his benign but effective weapon.

Dad liked to share with me anything he found beautiful or unusual. One day, he called me aside and said he had something he wanted me to see. I tagged along behind him, expecting to see a new hibiscus bloom, a pileated woodpecker, or perhaps a long-legged water bird stalking around. But he had something very different for me to admire. He stopped his journey through our yard, stepped aside, took me by the shoulders, and placed me eye to eye in front of a large spider with zigzags in its web. It was a "writing spider," and my father thought its black-and-gold geometric design was beautiful. But the surprise and shock of finding myself suddenly face to face with such a large and impressive spider was too much for me! I screamed and nearly ran over my father in my haste to leave. As I sped away, I caught a glimpse of his puzzled expression. I could tell he was thinking, *What's all the fuss? It's only a harmless spider, and a pretty one, at that!*

Although this encounter did not work out the way my dad hoped it would, it was one lesson in many that gave me the eyes of an artist. He trained me to see beauty everywhere, even in the smallest details. Now, I often stop to admire the vibrant colors and geometric designs on the jackets of small garden insects, the intricate designs of flowers, and the many shapes and textures of leaves and foliage. God's handiwork is truly amazing. I will always be grateful for this gift, for it has so enriched my life.

NEVER (HARDLY EVER) A DULL MOMENT

s a special treat during my preteen years, my father set up his canvas tent in our backyard for me and my two best friends, Frederica and Patsy. There, equipped with flashlights, chocolate bars, and comic books, we spent the night and had a grand time together. When the three of us were old enough for our feet to reach the brake pedal of a car, my father gave us all driving lessons. This happened when I was about eleven years old. These lessons took place on our spacious one-acre yard, and our vehicle was my father's hunting jeep. We leap-frogged around the yard a number of times before we learned how to gently ease the clutch in and out. My father was a good teacher who wanted to make sure I would be thoughtful of future passengers. He impressed upon me not to make any abrupt stops to avoid hurling my riders into the windshield!

My friends and I found plenty of entertainment on our acre of land. We had all the equipment for croquet, badminton, and table tennis, and we became very good at each of these pursuits. On our porch, an inviting hammock beckoned us, music was available through radio and record player, and in our living room was a baby grand piano. Mother played the piano by ear and, at one time, was a church organist. I took piano lessons for several years, as did my good friend Frederica. She and I had fun playing simple duets together. We knew them all.

We three friends were enamored by collies, and we read all of the Albert Payson Terhune books. When one of my dogs died in a car accident, my parents decided to do something very special for me. They wrote the Terhune family asking to buy one of their collie puppies. Mrs. Terhune wrote back and said their family did not believe in shipping their dogs and suggested that my parents look for one closer to home, which they did. (I still have the letter she wrote as a reminder of how kind and good my parents were to me.)

On the following Christmas, I awoke to the sounds of a yelping puppy. I rushed down the stairs to greet a tiny collie pup and joyfully gathered him into my arms. Unfortunately, my new little friend became ill and did not live very long. That is when a golden-colored cocker spaniel pup we named "Leo the Lion" became part of our lives, a gift from Frederica. Leo lived a long and happy life in our backyard, trapping green lizards, eating avocados, and occasionally devouring some of my father's prize plants. My father rarely lost his temper, but when Leo did away with twenty-five dollars' worth of newly installed bird of paradise plants, my father blew a fuse! Leo and I kept our distance from my father for about a week. On Leo's part, this was just canine wisdom. On my side, I wanted to make sure that Leo would remain part of our family.

Leo the Lion

ORCHID FEVER
IS CATCHING

ur gloriosa lilies, hibiscus, Don Juan red roses, gardenias, frangipani trees, blue agapanthus lilies, and birds of paradise brought us much pleasure. But our greatest floral joy came from the queen of flowers: the orchid. Orchids grew in the swampy lands and on the islands surrounding Tampa, and as we traveled around the state, we often encountered them in the wild. One variety especially captured our attention: the *Epidendrum tampense*, also known as the Florida Butterfly Orchid. Anchored by tenacious roots on oak tree limbs, these orchids send out tall shoots, each one graced by a tiny green and lavender flower. Orchids find oak trees to be very hospitable homes because they offer the perfect amount of filtered sunshine—50 percent.

When my parents joined the local Orchid Society, my father avidly began pursuing orchid culture. He ordered beautiful purple and lavender Cattleya orchids by the hundreds and stapled them to large slabs of Osmunda fiber (dense roots harvested from the Osmunda fern and sold to orchid growers as a growing medium). He then suspended them on a system of water pipes just outside our dining room windows. Over the pipes, he spread flexible green screen cloth that allowed only 50 percent of the sun to enter. Fertilization was accomplished by securing a bottle of fish oil to an outside tap and turning on the water so the pipes could spray a fine mist over the flowers. The orchids loved it and rewarded us with abundant blossoms.

When in bloom, the orchids on these large and heavy slabs could be transferred into our Florida room through open sliding glass doors by an extension rod that ran the length of the room. Once or twice a year when we had a freeze, we slid all of the orchids effortlessly down the pipes into our Florida room to remain until the weather warmed up. The trunk of an expired palm tree in the corner of our Florida room served to display more orchids. Amber and green-colored lights hidden beneath the foliage of our philodendron and elephant ear plants just outside our glass doors completed our pleasant ambience. Surrounded by such beauty, we enjoyed many evening meals in subtropical splendor.

In addition to our Cattleyas we grew Dancing Lady Orchids in square baskets made of wooden slats. The openness of the baskets gave plenty of room for the roots to expand and grow. One basket alone could hold as many as a hundred or more of these beautiful yellow blossoms.

As the first one in our household to get up in the morning, it fell to me each day to unlock and open the sliding glass doors into our Florida room. Taking a deep breath, I would inhale the intoxicating fragrance of a room filled with orchids. This was my daily aromatherapy.

Dad often shared his extensive orchid collection with friends. When one couple invited us to have dinner with them, my father selected a lovely orchid to give them. As he wrapped it, he had a flash of inspiration. From our tree, he picked a ripe avocado with its stem and a few leaves attached and secured the fruit to the orchid's main stem. Then off we went to see our friends. When presented with our gift, the wife believed what she saw and said to her husband, "Look, honey, this orchid has fruit! Isn't that amazing!" After they discovered my dad's little joke, they caught "orchid fever" and began their own collection, complete with a glass-enclosed greenhouse. Of course, this was immensely satisfying to my father.

13

HOW TO SUCCEED IN BUSINESS AND HAVE FUN AT THE SAME TIME

y father left school in the seventh grade and joined the work force after his father died. He claimed that mockingbirds were the cause of his departure. Through the open windows of his classroom, he heard their happy notes every day, inviting him to join them in the great out-of-doors. When he could resist their calls no longer, at the age of thirteen, he began his career as an independent businessman and became a student of life. To help support his family's income, he held a variety of interesting jobs. One of them was working behind the soda counter of Tibbet's Corner, the most popular drug store in Tampa at that time. There, he worked side by side with a new acquaintance, Laurens Jones, and the two became lifelong friends. They ate a lot of ice cream, and so did all their friends!

Armed with a recent six-week course in bookkeeping at a vocational school, Father confidently applied for a position as a bookkeeper at Firestone Tire & Rubber Company. They hired him. One month later, Mr. Acree, the store's office manager, could see that his novice worker needed some further training. He liked my father and began to mentor him and teach him everything he needed to know so he could stay on the job. Mr. Acree later became the district office manager of Firestone's Southeastern District, and he and my father remained friends for life.

My father eventually became a store manager and remained with Firestone for twenty-five years. He was a go-getter. His first store to manage, the smallest store in Firestone's Southeastern Region, was in Tampa. One year, he worked so hard that his tiny store captured the award for the most sales in the entire region. The prize provided a trip for two to see the World's Fair in New York City.

Several years later, Dad was transferred to Gainesville (137 miles to the north) to manage the store there. In Gainesville, he began to lay the foundation for his financial future. It all started with a small year-end bonus from Firestone, his employer.

DADDY'S CHRISTMAS
BONUS MULTIPLIES

y daddy's Christmas bonus from Firestone each year became lumber and paint that he used to build small black open trailers to sell. Everybody wanted one. He used the money from the trailers to buy land in Tampa. He then added a rental building so he could build more buildings until the whole block was filled with Daddy's buildings and he could put his feet up and collect the rent. It was a good plan, and it worked well for him.

Meanwhile, before someone came to claim the latest trailer, when Daddy removed the "For Sale" sign and hitched the trailer to the back of our car, it was transformed into a magic coach for all the children in the neighborhood. Dad drove the car, and we children rode in our open chariot down the road apiece, singing all the way until we reached a tiny creek. There, we gazed transfixed at the tiny bugs that skimmed across the surface of the water, small, motorized vessels that left imprinted lines in their wake. We hunted for sharks' teeth among the pebbles on the shore and beneath the surface of the clear water.

We rode on a little farther to a limestone sinkhole near Gainesville known as the Devil's Mill Hopper. It was deep, with slippery sides, and we descended carefully to the bottom on nature's staircase made of turquoise-blue clay. A stream ended its journey at the bottom as it cascaded over a rock ledge and mysteriously disappeared. There was just enough room for two small children to hide behind the waterfall and pretend they could not be seen. In the spring of the year, we picked violets.

Home again, when we children stepped down from our magic chariot, it became a simple small open trailer again, and the "For Sale" sign was repositioned on its back. But for my dad, the magic had just begun. These ordinary black trailers became a fleet of magic chariots that he rode in to make his dreams come true.

HOME SWEET HOME

fter three years in Gainesville, we moved back to Tampa and took up residence again on our acre of land. It was a minor adjustment for me, as I found two best friends right away in my fourth-grade classroom. Dad now owned almost one whole block of office buildings in the Palma Ceia business district. He opened a Firestone store in one of the buildings as an independent owner and hired friends and relatives to work for him. His business thrived. But eventually, with a change in the economy and so many mouths to feed (his employees), it became necessary to sell this store.

He wondered what to do next. It was to be an unusual choice.

THE BAR-G RANCH

ad's next major venture was to buy forty acres of land on the outskirts of Tampa and stock it with cattle. He had a friend who was a prosperous cattle rancher, and Dad thought he could do as well. Since he had no previous experience with ranching, he asked the friend to come with him to a cattle auction to help him select his herd. The two men had been at the auction for about a half an hour when my father asked his friend when he was going to start making bids. The friend replied, "I've already bought you fifty head!" Dad had not realized that when his friend scratched his ear or lifted an eyebrow or a finger, it was a bid! A Stetson cowboy hat became part of my father's wardrobe, and we observed that he was very comfortable with his new persona.

After the purchase of one hundred head of range cattle, a white-faced Hereford bull (very testy), an impressively tall white Brahma bull, complete with its signature hump, a horse, and a mule, we were in business, all of us. Dad was the rancher, and Mother and I were the ranch hands. Mother and I often were assigned the job of feeding this menagerie, and it was not a problem until one day, when the thundering herd did not stop to graze on the pellets we had thrown on the ground. The specter of that huge Brahma bull bearing down upon us, followed by a hundred or more head of cattle and a horse, inspired us. We instantly became Olympic athletes, dropped our feed sacks, ran for the fence, and leaped, barely ahead of the stampede. We were not even wearing red!

When one in the herd became ill, someone had to catch the steer so it could be treated. My parents worked it out this way: Mother would drive our jeep and give chase, and from the passenger side my father would try to rope the scurrying animal. This method worked quite well for them, and it was amusing to watch. Mother became an expert chaser of cattle over rough terrain, and Dad could sometimes rope a steer on his first try.

Then two things happened in the economy that conspired to produce yet another change in our lives. The price of beef cattle fell significantly, but the price of land skyrocketed. It was now time to sell our valuable forty acres of land and get out of the cattle business. Dad not only made money on this venture, he enhanced his already excellent reputation by adding cattle rancher and roping cowboy to his list of talents. It seemed that no matter what course he embarked upon, the Lord prospered him.

DAD GOES
BACK TO SCHOOL

ad's next adventure was to enroll in a real estate
course at Tampa University. At the same time, our
next-door neighbor, Chauncey Walker, was taking
an insurance course at the university. The two men
had their picture taken together wearing freshman
rat caps. Dad hung out his shingle on one of his own store buildings
and waited for the phone to ring. He had a manual typewriter and
did his own typing, hunt-and-peck style. When a lady called one day
and asked to speak to the personnel manager, Dad replied, "We don't
have a personnel manager; we don't have any personnel!"

It took a while for folks to find out he was in business. In the
meantime, he took an insurance course at Tampa University and
completed a course of study on the appraisal of real estate at the
University of Florida in Gainesville. He enjoyed these roles the best
of anything he had ever done. He always gave customers his very
best advice, whether or not it produced a sale. He saved money for
a lot of people and at the same made a good bit for himself. It was
all fun to him.

Occasionally, Dad was called upon by a local bank to conduct an estate sale of the contents of a house. He made the decision early on never to purchase any of the items that were for sale. He valued his integrity and wanted others to value it, as well. As a result, he became known for his honesty and professionalism. One day, after conducting one of these estate sales, my dad and a bank manager were walking through a now empty house. They came upon the only item left over, a nice-looking brass pot with a missing handle.

My father asked the manager how much he would sell it for.

The man replied, "One dollar."

My dad pulled out a one-dollar bill and reached down for the pot. Inside he found the missing handle.

In mock dismay, the manager said, "Wish I'd seen that!"

Dad replied, "I'll sell it to you for a dollar."

The manager allowed my father to keep the pot, the only item he ever purchased from one of these sales. It resides in my home today. Still beautiful, it stands as a reminder of my dad's uncompromising principles.

A GOOD WOMAN

o far, I have written much about my dad and not much yet about my mom. This is probably because Dad was the undisputed star of our family and the life of the party wherever he went. Mother adored him, as did I, and the three of us had a grand time together. Dad was the spice, and Mother was the sweetness.

Mom had two brothers, Byron and Jimmy, and the three were raised by their grandmother, Mary Miller Morgan, a dear lady who survived the Civil War years in Alabama before moving to Florida. She took on her three grandchildren to raise when she was in her late sixties. They lived one block from Tampa's Bayshore Drive before the seawall was built, when the water in the bay was clear and fine for swimming. Byron and Jim had a canoe, and the three siblings paddled all over the bay together. Although they were really her aunts and uncles, her grandmother's large family of children became like sisters and brothers to my mom. Since most of them remained in the Tampa area, we were blessed with lots of close family ties. I have my great-grandmother's name, Mary Miller. This became significant for me later on in life. Just like she did, I married a pastor, and when I moved to Brazil with my new husband, I found Miller relatives there. Great-Grandmother's uncle, Irvin Louis Miller, emigrated to Brazil after the Civil War and left there a huge family, all of them my Brazilian cousins.

Mom taught elementary school in the Hillsborough County School System until my dad was transferred by Firestone to manage one of their stores in West Palm Beach. There she became the organist for one of the churches in the city. Soon after, I made my appearance, and we became a threesome. When my parents eventually returned to Tampa, Mother again became closely involved with family and friends. One of her great joys was membership in a garden club to which many of our family belonged. My dad was a popular speaker at the club. He took many slide pictures of flowers and liked to "wow" people with his knowledge of all their precise botanical names.

Everyone considered Mom an excellent cook. I remember with great nostalgia her roast beef and gravy, prime ribs, stuffed squash topped with bacon, banana cakes, crescent cookies, and tapioca pudding. My friends often asked me for her recipes. When I think of the three meals that she provided for us every day, I wonder how she could have done this happily for so many years. Mother was good to me in every possible way, and we had a chance to become closer than ever when illness made it necessary for her to leave Florida and come to live in Atlanta near me.

My dad once made this comment: "You can never repay your parents." He was thinking about his own parents at the time, but I can certainly attest to the truth of this statement as I apply it to my own two parents. They are irreplaceable, and I will be forever grateful to them. Because of their love and provision for me, my early years were lived in Paradise.

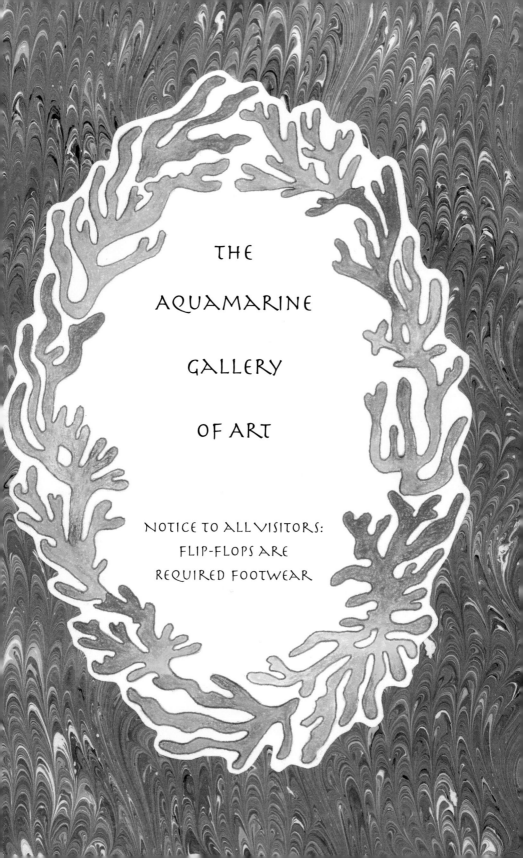

THE

AQUAMARINE

GALLERY

OF ART

NOTICE TO ALL VISITORS:
FLIP-FLOPS ARE
REQUIRED FOOTWEAR

Aquamarine Universe
Watercolor

WEST COAST LOVE

O magical sand with sparkle and shine,
You speak to me of another time
When hearts were young and cares were few,
Shells were many, and parents were two.

A shoreline cottage was our favorite vacation.
Simple pleasures were our recreation.
Wind sang through Australian Pines,
Peace was there and peace was mine.

Blue-green waters, calm and clear,
Warmed by the Gulf Stream flowing near,
Made dancing waves in the breeze,
Refreshing to bathers in the salty sea.

When still the wind and slow the tide,
You could see way down where little fish hide.
Turning and darting, as if on command,
Together they weaved in a silent band.

Below the clear water in a mirrored pool,
A rippled sand carpet lay soft and smooth.
Wiggle your toes and you would uncover a prize:
A prickly sand dollar or snaillike cat's eyes.

A rare lion's paw might also be found
Together with small shells in a large mound.
As we searched for hidden treasures,
Anticipation was half the pleasure.

Sea gulls pranced up and down the shore
As pelicans above hungrily soared,
Diving headlong into the deep
To surface again with fish in beak.

The rocking motion of the waves
Calmed our nerves if they were frayed.
Swimming gave us a good appetite
And helped us to sleep soundly at night.

We rode those waves in our big inner tubes
Then dined on fried chicken and sweet tea with ice cubes.
When the mullet were jumping, our poles went taut.
Seafood is much better when it has just been caught.

The little coquinas that burrowed in the sand,
We'd gather up with a sieve by hand.
They made a tasty delicate stew,
And their shells provided artwork for us to do.

I am glad these memories are still intact.
So, when I need to, I can go back
And capture anew my childhood bliss,
Find joy again when life seems amiss.

The ocean, so generous with its gifts,
Delights us, feeds us, and gives us a lift.
It soothes and heals us of our stress.
From sunrise to sunset, it is designed to bless.

GENESIS OF WEST COAST LOVE

t was one of those nights when I couldn't get to sleep no matter what remedies I tried. Nothing seemed to work, not even chamomile tea and warm milk. My thoughts became an intrusive parade of life's latest challenges, all demanding my immediate attention. Then I tried something different. I searched for a time in my life when everything was as close to perfect as this life can be. I thought that if I could remember such a place and time I could recapture and tap into the joys that accompanied me then with a peaceful and good night's sleep to follow.

It didn't take long to find such a place. I traveled to Florida on Memory Lane and stopped my train of thought at Indian Rocks Beach, one of the Gulf beaches near Tampa. I disembarked at our family's favorite vacation cottage right on the beach. My parents were then young and lively, and I was at an age young enough to have not a care in the world.

There was much to delight in this simple setting. Air-conditioning for our cottage was provided by cool gulf breezes through windows that actually could be opened. And with an open window, one can be lulled to sleep by the soothing sounds of the surf. No vacuum cleaner was provided—just a broom to sweep out the sand. The warm gulf waters were just a few steps away from our screened-in porch. I pictured myself seated at the water's edge, sorting through an array of shells, picking up handfuls of pure white beach sand, and letting the sand sift through my open fingers. With the sun's reflection, each tiny crystal of sand shimmered and sparkled on its downward path. To me, the effect was magical, and I felt again the joy of that moment in time. But sleep still eluded me as the words of this poem came to life. So, I arose and wrote them down. Many more such poems followed, always thereafter inspired by the love that I have for my home state of Florida and the joy that my life there brought to me so many years ago.

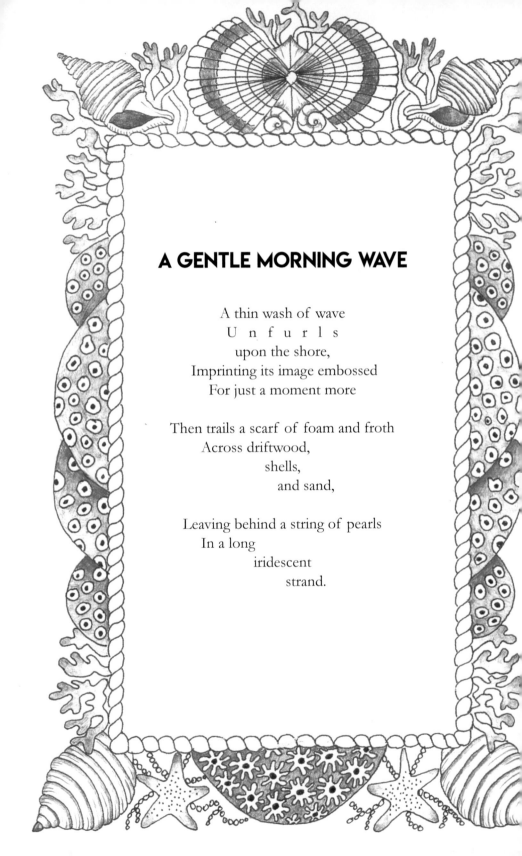

A GENTLE MORNING WAVE

A thin wash of wave
U n f u r l s
upon the shore,
Imprinting its image embossed
For just a moment more

Then trails a scarf of foam and froth
Across driftwood,
shells,
and sand,

Leaving behind a string of pearls
In a long
iridescent
strand.

Florida Girl
Watercolor
by Alice J. Walker

FLORIDA GIRL

I visited my home state in the spring of the year
And discovered anew many things I hold dear.
A mockingbird greeted me and began to sing
Its repertoire of songs that herald the spring.

A floating splash of color in the garden caught my eye.
It was my favorite Lepidoptera: the Zebra butterfly.
Underneath the oak tree, orchids were in bloom.
I saw a Great Blue Heron from our living room.

Next came a walk outdoors with a gentle light breeze,
And soon I was writing these words that you see.
I'm a Florida Girl, and I'm hard to please,
For I grew up with the sun and fell in love with the breeze.

Oranges grew at my own backdoor.
With papayas and mangos, there was fruit galore.
In March, the scent of orange blossoms filled the air,
For these wonderful trees grew everywhere.

When it rains in Florida, the sun still shines,
So, with cooling showers, a rainbow rises.
In the late evening comes our tropical moon,
A golden orb in the month of June.

The mockingbird's song is a rare melody,
For the music it sings in Florida is unique,
As its songs do vary from state to state
And change with the birds that it imitates.

Sometimes they will surprise you with a concert at night,
Singing glorious melodies that bring such delight.
And in the spring when their joy is complete,
They can turn flips in the air and still land on their feet.

When winter comes to visit each year
It stays a few weeks and then disappears.
Along the way it discards the snow,
The chilly winds, and temperatures low.

We could venture outdoors most every day
To visit our nearby beaches and bays.
I loved the smell of salt water, the lapping of the waves,
The mild temperatures at night, the pleasant warm days.

At low tide, the gulf was calm and serene,
Its placid waters transparent blue-green.
But after a storm, or sometimes late at night,
The waves would crash in with power and might.

The harbor sounds of Tampa we often did hear,
Especially in the cooler fall of the year,
The muted sounds of an occasional barge
Or the deep-toned horns of freighters large.

These were all ships entering our port,
Bringing their various cargos ashore.
Harbor activities were busy after dark
And made an interesting place for folks to park.

Spotlights surrounded the large ships' holds
As channel waters lapped at concrete seawalls.
Commands echoed across water, directing crews,
Telling them what they needed to do.

At night, Bayshore lights arranged in a curve
Were called, by my mother, her string of pearls.
And years ago, when the lamplights were gas,
My father lit them with a tall stick and a match.

These memories of Florida are now history,
But as I live them again, joy comes to me.
I'm still the happiest when it's eighty degrees.
If it gets any colder, I just might freeze.
I'm a Florida Girl and I'm hard to please!

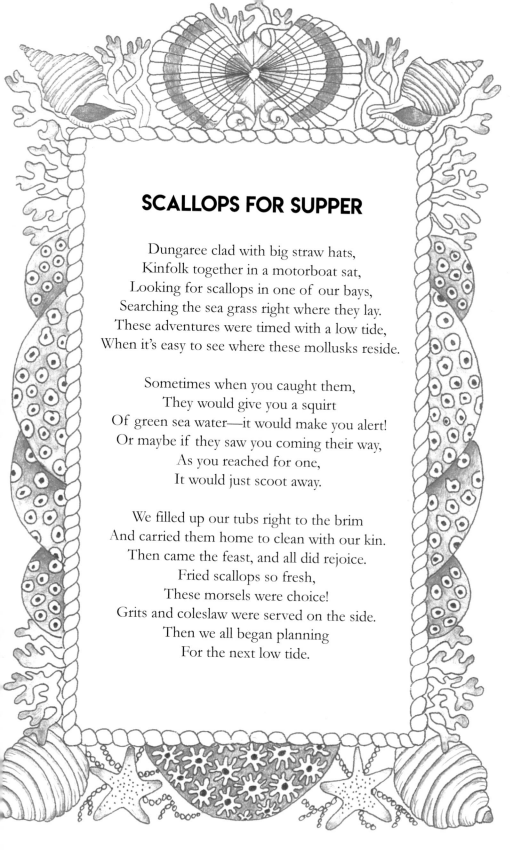

SCALLOPS FOR SUPPER

Dungaree clad with big straw hats,
Kinfolk together in a motorboat sat,
Looking for scallops in one of our bays,
Searching the sea grass right where they lay.
These adventures were timed with a low tide,
When it's easy to see where these mollusks reside.

Sometimes when you caught them,
They would give you a squirt
Of green sea water—it would make you alert!
Or maybe if they saw you coming their way,
As you reached for one,
It would just scoot away.

We filled up our tubs right to the brim
And carried them home to clean with our kin.
Then came the feast, and all did rejoice.
Fried scallops so fresh,
These morsels were choice!
Grits and coleslaw were served on the side.
Then we all began planning
For the next low tide.

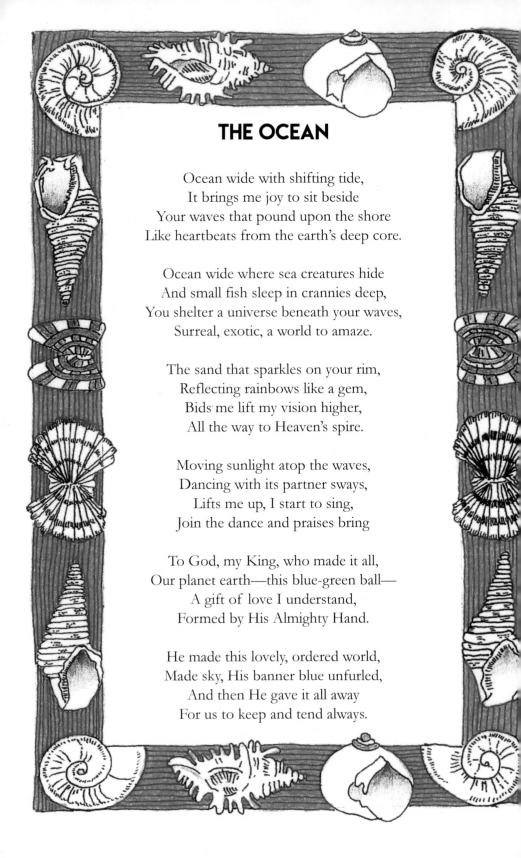

THE OCEAN

Ocean wide with shifting tide,
It brings me joy to sit beside
Your waves that pound upon the shore
Like heartbeats from the earth's deep core.

Ocean wide where sea creatures hide
And small fish sleep in crannies deep,
You shelter a universe beneath your waves,
Surreal, exotic, a world to amaze.

The sand that sparkles on your rim,
Reflecting rainbows like a gem,
Bids me lift my vision higher,
All the way to Heaven's spire.

Moving sunlight atop the waves,
Dancing with its partner sways,
Lifts me up, I start to sing,
Join the dance and praises bring

To God, my King, who made it all,
Our planet earth—this blue-green ball—
A gift of love I understand,
Formed by His Almighty Hand.

He made this lovely, ordered world,
Made sky, His banner blue unfurled,
And then He gave it all away
For us to keep and tend always.

Listen close to wind and wave,
The musical voices of God at play.
He speaks to us in many ways,
But were there words I think He would say:

"I love you, children of My heart.
I died for you to impart
My joy and peace and love so great.
So, come to me and do not wait.

"Your Father, God, loves you so.
I made this world for you to know
The height of love, its width and breadth
Proved to all by My death.

"My creation speaks for me.
It needs no words, just eyes to see
And ears to hear its melody.
Then take My love and free forever be."

Ocean wide where seashells preside,
Where dolphins roll and pelicans dive,
You offer a world for us to explore,
An aquamarine gallery at the seashore.

"Yonder is the sea, great and wide
Filled with countless creatures
Living things both small and great."
—Psalm 104:25

TRIBUTE TO OCEAN WAVES

 t was time for a long overdue visit to our Florida west coast beaches, and I could hardly wait! I needed an ocean tranquilizer.

We parked beside a lighthouse and made our way through scrub palmettos and tall sand dunes to reach the shore. The minute I saw the ocean and heard the waves, my joy could not be contained. Filling the air with shouts of praise, I paced back and forth on the shore giving the ocean a standing ovation. As I clapped my hands and called for encores, the waves graciously responded. I absorbed as many repeats as we had time, and left filled to the brim with the joy that always accompanies visits to my friend, the Ocean.

ENCORE

Whenever I walk
   along the shore
I cry out to each wave

"Encore! Encore!"

The waves then oblige
As they surge with the
      tide
And there is always time
   for one more

Mary Renshaw

43

WEST COAST MATINEE

To the evening beach come Florida fans
To watch coastal sunsets from armchairs of sand.
Folks quietly gather for a heavenly display
Near the water's edge at the close of day.

God paints a panorama with holy beams of light
And mobiles of clouds drifting left and right.
Each canvas is a masterpiece with bold celestial hues.
Burnt orange, crimson, and violet darken into midnight blue.

If you have missed the latest shows,
There is no need for sorrow.
Although there are no reruns,
There will be a better one tomorrow.

This matinee is free, and there's plenty of room.
Join the terns and seagulls that line up to see it, too.
If earth reflects such beauty on an ordinary day,
Just think what God has planned for us
In that life across the bay!

        The   The
   heavens   vault
     tell   of
    out   heaven
    the   reveals
  Glory   His
    of   handi-
   God   work

—Psalm 19:1, NEB

44

SUBTROPICAL DREAMS

Seeking peace, I close my eyes—
Transported, awake in paradise
On a subtropical isle where I am mesmerized
By a garden framed in colored lights.
There is a cool sea breeze
On a warm summer night.

The garden is painted in rich dark greens.
Philodendron leaves are the background screen.
Upon the stage are the beauty queens:
Dancing Lady Orchids dressed in yellow and green.
Backstage, Birds of Paradise flock together,
Ready to perform in any kind of weather.

Palm fronds rustle gently in the breeze,
Casting evening shadows that change constantly.
A mockingbird sings his nighttime melody.
I hear the distant waves—the rhythm of the sea.
"What a pleasant place to rest," I say, and settle in a chair
To enjoy the summer night and my peace to repair.

Then the memories return,
Scenes of days so warm and fair.
I'm a Florida girl once more,
Wearing flowers in my hair,
Walking barefoot on the sand,
Enjoying the sunshine, and wearing a tan.

Harbor lights on summer nights
Were a string of pearls twinkling bright.
Distant buoys rang in the bay,
Helping helmsmen to find their way.

The deep-toned horns of freighters large
And softer sounds of a smaller barge
Were sounds heard often in the night,
Their nautical music always a delight.

Twice daily came the seagulls, laughing in the sky,
Crossing from bay to bay, conversing as they fly.
The egret-ibis-herring-cranes, which one it's hard to say,
With stilt-like fragile legs and feathers of white and gray,
Stalked through marshes, ponds, and lakes,
Using sword-sharp beaks to spear their prey.

We beachcombed on nearby islands,
Cuban sandwiches were our lunch.
Then we watched the dolphins roll
And laughed as the mullets jumped.
I lived a barefoot life; flip-flops were my shoes.
Time for me stood still until one day, I moved.

I left my footprints in the sand;
Though waves removed their trace,
Memories remained, never to be erased.
What is the call of the ocean to me,
Of a former life beside the sea,
And all the people once dear to me?

Speak to me, ocean! Speak to me, sea!
What is this magic that you have over me?
Truly, I would like to know
Why is it that I love you so?
I'll listen for your answer clear,
Why it is that I hold you dear.

SEASIDE MYSTERY

Child of the ocean, lover of the sea,
Think it not strange that I speak to thee.
Ocean's daughter you became,
When my waves called your name.
There are reasons why you feel as you do.
Sit here beside me, and I'll tell you a few.

At water's edge, you may build
Sandcastles with a moat to fill.
A mangrove pencil washed ashore
Can inscribe your name and more,
A message on the moistened sand,
In any chosen calligraphic hand.

Seaside visits can repair
Your health with my ionic air.
Cool sea breezes that refresh
Accompany your siesta's rest.
And if you cannot sleep at night,
The rhythm of my waves will put that right.

My daily tidal ebb and flow
Uncovers treasures from below.
Flotsam, jetsam, driftwood, shells
Arrive with every tidal swell.
I cast them freely on the shore,
Lay them at your feet to be explored.

Sailboats and surfers ride my waves.
Swimmers relax in my embrace.
Each day, new paintings can be seen
On my horizon's wide-angle screen.
At each sunset, beach fans line up in rows,
Ready to enjoy these picture shows.

Need I mention catching fish?
Red snapper makes a tasty dish!
Fresh scallops caught in a nearby bay
Are sweet and delicious, I hear folks say.
Smoked mullet, crab cakes, and shrimp scampi,
These menu choices make everyone happy.

Now look beyond the joys I revealed.
Go past the happiness that you feel
And ask the fish who painted their scales.
Do you know who designed the whale,
Who set boundaries of my waters deep,
Saying, "Stop here, don't overreach"?

Who planned the seabird's wings?
How did the mockingbird learn to sing?
When you observe my ocean blue,
With its aquamarine and indigo hues,
Can you imagine The Artist Great,
Dipping His brush in watercolor paint?

When you can answer these questions for me,
You will know why you love the sea.
The hand of the Lord created me
And all the fish that swim in the sea.
He taught the birds how to sing
And gave to them their useful wings.

He crafted an infinite number of shells,
Used geometric designs drawn quite well.
He painted shallow waters a transparent light green.
Farther out they become aquamarine.
Above the ocean deep, they turn indigo blue.
Then He added sunrise and sunset just for you!

Surveying God's amazing creation
Brings joy and calls for celebration.
His majestic and awesome design
Reveals to all His Glory Divine.
This is the reason that you love me.
I am a part of God's great mystery.

How I wish

That somewhere

There existed an

I S L A N D

For those that are

WISE and of

GOOD WILL

 - Albert Einstein

Treasure Island
Watercolor Illustration

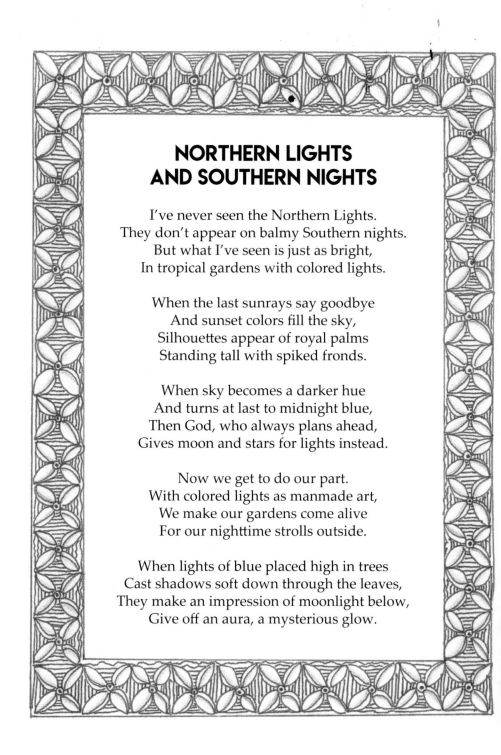

NORTHERN LIGHTS
AND SOUTHERN NIGHTS

I've never seen the Northern Lights.
They don't appear on balmy Southern nights.
But what I've seen is just as bright,
In tropical gardens with colored lights.

When the last sunrays say goodbye
And sunset colors fill the sky,
Silhouettes appear of royal palms
Standing tall with spiked fronds.

When sky becomes a darker hue
And turns at last to midnight blue,
Then God, who always plans ahead,
Gives moon and stars for lights instead.

Now we get to do our part.
With colored lights as manmade art,
We make our gardens come alive
For our nighttime strolls outside.

When lights of blue placed high in trees
Cast shadows soft down through the leaves,
They make an impression of moonlight below,
Give off an aura, a mysterious glow.

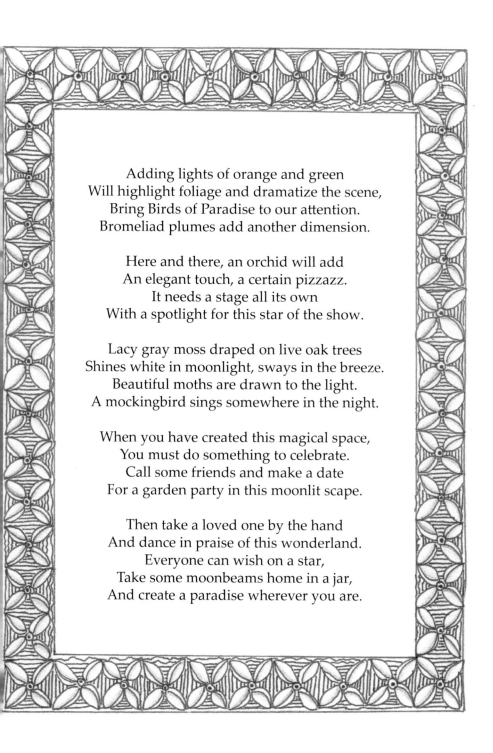

Adding lights of orange and green
Will highlight foliage and dramatize the scene,
Bring Birds of Paradise to our attention.
Bromeliad plumes add another dimension.

Here and there, an orchid will add
An elegant touch, a certain pizzazz.
It needs a stage all its own
With a spotlight for this star of the show.

Lacy gray moss draped on live oak trees
Shines white in moonlight, sways in the breeze.
Beautiful moths are drawn to the light.
A mockingbird sings somewhere in the night.

When you have created this magical space,
You must do something to celebrate.
Call some friends and make a date
For a garden party in this moonlit scape.

Then take a loved one by the hand
And dance in praise of this wonderland.
Everyone can wish on a star,
Take some moonbeams home in a jar,
And create a paradise wherever you are.

ISLAND EXCURSION

Once in a while, an island excursion
Made for us an exciting diversion.
We'd pack up a lunch, take a small radio,
Add towels and swimsuits, then off we would go.

Steering our boat against the tide,
Bouncing over the waves on our ride,
We passed by islands of nesting birds
As cool ocean spray showered our clothes.

A bit offshore, we anchored the boat,
Jumped overboard, and tossed out the rope.
With picnic basket to shoreline we'd wade,
Heading for palm trees and plenty of shade.

The beaches were combed, searched up and down.
Trophies were gathered, and treasures were found.
Lanterns and bottles in perfect condition
Made for our bay home a "just right" addition.

We found driftwood, corks, and a few seashells
As we listened to buoys ring their faraway bells.
A swim, then lunch and a nap were enjoyed,
And next on the list was a special reward.

For some time, my father had planned
To introduce me to this remote island.
"Daughter, do come along with me.
There is something nearby I want you to see."

He drew back a curtain of vines and brush.
We stepped into a clearing with a holy hush.
We found ourselves on a leaf-strewn rise,
'Neath a majestic live oak, its arms opened wide.

The stage was deserted, quiet and still,
Save for a spider spinning its silk,
Basking in a spotlight of the bright sun's shaft,
Performing all alone its aerial act.

Approaching the oak tree, I became quite aware
Of a delightful fragrance filling the air.
Moving closer, then I could see
Wild orchids abloom covering the tree.

Their beautiful faces were an artist's delight
Of delicate colors and elegant lines.
I stood there a long time just taking it in.
When would I see such a scene again?

We picked one orchid to take away
As a special memory of that day,
And then it was that I received this message
A gift for my life—a father's blessing.

"Daughter, I wanted you to see this place
And the hidden beauty that is yours to take,
It's all around you—the wonder of life.
I hope you will look for it as long as you live.

"It's a beautiful world if you have eyes to see.
This is the inheritance that you have from me.
Decide to have fun your whole life through,
And in the process others will, too.

"Each day we are alive is a precious gift.
Make the most of each one so it gives you a lift!"
At last it was time for us to go,
And we said goodbye to our wild orchid show.

But we had one last joy as we went on our way,
And it seemed the right touch for the end of our day.
As we turned our boat around, away from the shore,
We had a last glimpse of the Tampa harbor.

Overhead, the sky was ablaze
With orange, violet, and the last sunrays.
Then too soon these colors faded away
On the fast-changing canvas over the bay.

Twilight came softly and slowly revealed
Bayshore lights from afar as a long string of pearls.
Then safe in our cottage and ready for sleep,
We settled down to enjoy pleasant dreams.

When I look at these joys through the lens of time,
They take on a quality quite sublime.
I love to pluck them from memory's file
And savor each one for just a short while.

These days are now gone, but I have memories
That will live on forever in my reverie.
My love for Florida will never fade,
For I have seen her beauty in full display.

Beach Boardwalk
Colored-Pencil Illustration

I STILL LOVE YOU

My beloved's voice calls to me
Over sand dunes, through palm trees,
In familiar sounds of restless waves.
"I still love you!" I hear myself say.

Passion mine, blue and green,
With frothy ribbons trailed in streams,
Holds out curved arms to me.
I race for the embrace of my sea.

I've been away far too long!
Hold me in your current strong,
Let me breathe your briny air,
Make seaweed bows atop your hair.

We'll make love with a salty kiss.
Stress is gone, replaced by bliss.
I give myself, my heart, to thee,
My blue-green, restless, liquid sea.

Playful friend, tossing me about
With tidal tugs—I give a gleeful shout
And tumble sideways across a sandy bar
To rest until the next wave carries me afar.

I touch eternity when I'm with you.
My spirit life is then renewed,
And even though I've wandered far,
I still feel part of all you are.

THE SEA REPLIES

Your parents placed you in my arms
When you were a babe of three.
Together you played games with me,
Happy child of sand and sea.

Now they are gone—I miss them too.
But you are not alone—I share their love for you.
They crossed my vast expanse at sunset
Then climbed a moonbeam stair

To claim a better life among the stars,
Live anew in a far celestial sphere.
Don't forget that sunset is not the end, my dear.
The sun itself moves along to another hemisphere.

They too will shine and glow
In different ways from those you know.
Come to visit often—listen—hear,
And I will remind you of those happy years.

They would be glad to know
That often when you think of them,
You offer thanks and praise to Him
Who set us on this earth a-spin.

Until you join them in the stars,
I'll be your special friend.
We'll play once more on Florida shores.
Your restless heart, I'll mend.

I knew you'd travel far and wide,
Find other loves than me besides,
But my arms are always open wide.
I'm here for you when you decide.
I still love you.

BEACH MAN

eachcombing can be a never-ending source of fascination for anyone. Driftwood, bleached fish bones, seedpods, rocks, beach glass, sharks' teeth, and shells can turn a walk on the beach into a delightful treasure hunt. My radar is always on during these strolls, and so it was, even up until the last minute on the way to our car one summer afternoon in Florida. My family and I had spent a delightful day at Fort De Soto Park near St. Petersburg's Sunshine Skyway, and my sack of treasures was nearly full. Even so, I was still scanning on the way to our car when I spotted a very unusual rock. It was a tiny, perfectly shaped little rectangle that the ocean had sculpted into a face. Not to be outdone, my husband looked around and found a rock he thought was just as interesting. It obviously had spent a lot of time in some rough ocean water, and that is just what made it so attractive! When I placed the two rocks together and added two conch shells for legs, Beach Man came to life!

Upon a close examination of my newly created sculpture, I found the likeness of two hands and well-developed shoulder muscles that suggested Beach Man had been working out at the gym for a very long time. I decided to immortalize him in a color pencil portrait.

Although not beautiful in the usual sense of the word, Beach Man is dear to my heart. He came to life in my hands. He has become, for me, a friend and a spokesperson whose task it is to promote the pursuit of beachcombing by dramatizing our considerable powers of creativity and imagination. Beach Man tells us, "When you visit the beach, look around and be alert, for you never know what is beyond the next sand dune or around the next curve in the shore."

Beach Man
Colored-Pencil Illustration

A FRIENDLY BAYSIDE RETREAT

A plain and simple cottage on Indian Rocks Beach
Was an oasis of quiet at a friend's bayside retreat.
It was a place to relax—"Welcome, do come in!"
Bare feet were acceptable; our vacation could begin.

No telephone was there to disturb our peace,
Just the laughing gulls exchanging pleasantries.
We left the doors wide open—they said it was okay,
But a heron could stroll in, wanting to investigate.

Fans overhead kept us nice and cool,
And the nearby Gulf was a warm swimming pool.
A friendly sea breeze rustled through palm fronds
To further cool us off before it moved along.

Often came a visitor stepping gingerly,
A snow-white egret with bright-yellow feet.
We carefully avoided his long sharp beak
As this curious bird looked for something to eat.

A writing desk awaited us with a view of the bay.
A tall black stove stood by for chilly winter days.
There were books on bird-watching and identifying stars.
Fishing poles were handy; straw hats hung on the wall.

The house offered games to play and a round Frisbee.
An outside shower washed off our sandy feet.
We found comfortable chairs on the shady front porch.
Two bicycles were there to ride; who could ask for more?

Friends shared their home with us.
It was so nice to see.
Simple pleasures are the best.
They are all we need.

Seaside Retreat
Watercolor
by Frederica Newsome

ISLAND DISCOVERY

Exploring islands is my greatest pleasure.
The joy that it gives me is far beyond measure,
For I love to swim and lie on the sand,
Walk down the beach with my love hand in hand,

See the sailboats glide smoothly by,
Watch the pelicans soar through the sky,
Hear the cry of seagulls high in the air,
Hear the pounding surf, feel the wind in my hair,

See the sunsets light up the sky,
Watch the bright colors fade, then slowly die.
All of these things I like very well,
But what I love most is finding seashells.

Now, shell collecting is not for everyone.
As for me, I would say it is serious fun,
So just any island won't do for me,
And my research was done quite carefully.

I had to look for many a day,
Question beachcombers to hear what they would say.
Then I visited each island in order to see
Which of them my favorite would be.

At last, I found my island remote,
With its large banks of seashells and tall sea oats.
There was a friendly wave at the toll keeper's gate
And a lighthouse on a point to investigate.

The bicycle path was inviting to me
And the summer theatre with its shows to see.
There were stretches of beach with no houses at all,
And those that were there were cottages small.

They were landscaped with palmettos and cabbage palms,
Sea grapes on sand dunes and morning glories for lawns.
Australian pines were lined up by the sea,
Their thick brown carpets spread out beneath the trees.

I knew very soon it was a place I could stay,
That would hold my interest day after day.
But what really caught my eye
Were all the shells washed up by the tide.

I have now learned a secret, and I'll tell it to you.
If you want shells, this is what you must do:
Look for a beach with some shells rather rare,
Of the sort that you don't find just anywhere.

And although the best ones be scattered and few,
And some of these be broken in two,
If there are enough of the rarer kind,
You will know to return at another time.

For I had this promise given to me,
Borne by the voice of the wind and the sea:
"Come back," they said, "after a storm,
And come the next day at early morn.

"For there will be others just like you,
Looking for shells all shiny and new.
A harvest then you will reap from the sea
Of better shells than these that you see.

"You must wait for strong winds and a forceful tide
To uncover new shells and give them a ride,
Then finally deposit them high up on land
To await the collector's reaching hand.

"The new ones will be perfect, whole and unmarred,
Deeply colored, and without chip or scar.
But come early, or you'll miss out,
For there will be others scouting about!"

At last, my visit came to an end,
And I waved goodbye to my gatekeeper friend.
But I vowed to come back on another day
When there would be time for an overnight stay,

For I knew that the island had spoken to me
Of a friendship between us that yet may be,
As I dreamed of picnics and bicycle rides,
Moonlight strolls on the beach at low tide,

Drifting to sleep with the sounds of the surf,
To wake in the morning for a swim in the gulf,
Then diving into a large shell mound,
Sure that treasures soon would be found,

Afternoon naps in the heat of the day,
A good book to read, some games to play,
Fresh-caught fish for dinner each night,
Served with tropical fruit, a menu delight.

But should I never see my island again,
I'll remember it well in my daydreams,
For it can never really be lost to me.
I can travel any time through memories to
GASPARILLA ISLAND, FLORIDA

A MORE FORTUNATE DESTINY

IT IS PERHAPS A MORE FORTUNATE DESTINY TO HAVE A TASTE FOR COLLECTING SHELLS THAN TO BE BORN A MILLIONAIRE

R.L. Stevenson

Fishing Lines

BEACH

THE FISH HOUSE

n the 1970s, my parents built a retirement cottage on lower Tampa Bay. Their modest, two-bedroom A-frame had a great view of the many islands that speckled the bay. My father called it "The Fish House." Here they happily spent a part of every week.

The waters in this part of Tampa Bay were known as excellent fishing grounds. My parents spent four days a week away from city life, enjoying the peace and quiet of nature and the anticipation of daily fish dinners. The Sunshine Skyway Bridge joining St. Petersburg and Bradenton was visible on most days, as well as Tampa's Bayshore Drive in the far distance. These views became especially beautiful all lit up at night. Since we were so close to the harbor entrance, we often saw ocean liners and freighters coming and going. I enjoyed hearing their boat horns breaking the silence on foggy nights.

Of course, with a fishing cottage, one needs a boat. And a dock. And some fishing gear. This was all that was necessary, because the fish were biting most of the time. At times, it seemed that the fish were challenging us to come and get them, because we often saw mullet jumping straight up out of the water in front of our cottage! The more acrobatic ones would occasionally do backflips. Some theorize that mullet jump because predators are pursuing them. Others claim that they jump just for fun. But the strangest explanation is that they are seeking aerial respiration. Mullet are bottom feeders in the daytime, and if they are in areas of low oxygen concentration they may need to replenish the oxygen supply in their system. We never knew for certain what prompted them to display this odd behavior, but it sure captured our attention. A group of friendly dolphins often joined this show, expressing their joy in this excellent environment by rolling and frolicking in the waters in front of our cottage. We had plenty of entertainment in our very own water park.

Water birds roosted on small mangrove islands within sight of our cottage. My father invited a group of bird-watching friends to cruise these islands with him to observe the various bird rookeries. At that time, south Tampa Bay was an unspoiled and virtually pristine area of nature's beauty and bounty.

One of these offshore islands held an extra fascination for my father. Upon exploration, he and his best friend discovered there an Indian mound. It claimed their attention because they noticed a higher elevation in the middle of the island. The Indians liked these higher sites because they offered protection and served as lookouts. These two adventurers made many trips to their secret island to collect trophies. Upon the mound, they found potsherds (broken pottery), clam shells left over from the Indians' shellfish dinners, arrowheads in perfect condition, and a nice sampling of their more sophisticated weapons, such as clubs and axe-heads. Most of these items were later donated to the Tampa Historical Society for others to enjoy and dream about having adventures of their own.

My favorite bayside occupation was island hopping and beach-combing. These offshore islands were rarely visited, as the main attraction in that area was the lure of catching fish. Each year, Tampa celebrates the Gasparilla Festival, named after the pirate José Gaspar who patrolled these areas. On these visits, we could always hope to uncover some gold doubloons. This never happened, but many other delightful articles were added to our treasure trove. We lucked upon several ships' lanterns and found many interesting pieces of drift-wood useful for flower arrangements. There were colorful bottles, rare seashells, and unexpected surprises wrapped up in seaweed. Add to that an island picnic, a swim in the bay, and, if we were lucky, some fish caught for supper on the way back home. This was such a satisfying and delightful pastime for me that I still daydream about these beautiful island adventures.

The Fish House
Ruskin, Florida

FISH INSURANCE

y father sold fish insurance. This is what he told his guests who accompanied him on fishing excursions. It was more like a guarantee to the participants that they would absolutely and without fail catch fish. There was a reason for his extraordinary confidence. He had discovered a place where fish were always in abundance. He shared his secret with only a select few, one of them being his best friend, Laurens Jones.

Laurens, an estate lawyer, often worked with the trust department of a large downtown Tampa bank. Occasionally, new trust officers would join the bank's staff, and they usually came from inland northern states. Laurens and my father took it upon themselves to indoctrinate these new arrivals to Florida's west coast. Their plan was to invite several at a time to go fishing. The men would always want to help out with the plans by offering to bring lunch. "That won't be necessary," my father would say, "for we will have fresh-caught fish for our lunch."

"But what if we don't catch anything?" the men protested.

"Shouldn't we take along some sandwiches, just in case?" Then my father would inform them that he "sold" fish insurance, which came with a guarantee that fish would always be caught. Reluctantly, the men would put aside plans to bring reserve sandwiches, deciding instead to throw themselves upon the mercy of the captain of the fishing boat.

Besides the necessary fishing gear, supplies to prepare lunch were a cast-iron skillet, some cooking oil, salt, several avocados, and the *tar kettle*, a metal coffeepot so named because of its blackened condition after sitting atop so many island-made fires. There was also a bottle of bourbon for a small after-lunch nip.

The chosen area was always off the coast of Tarpon Springs and Dunedin, where there are three islands: Caladesi Island, Honeymoon Island, and Anclote Key. Honeymoon and Caladesi were once one large island until the hurricane of 1921 split it in two, forming Hurricane Pass with Caladesi Island to the south. The more northerly island became known as Honeymoon Island after a New York developer sponsored a contest for newlyweds in 1939. Fifty palm-thatched bungalows were built, and fifty lucky couples won two-week subtropical getaways.

The Dunedin Causeway, built in 1964, connected Honeymoon Island to the mainland. The state of Florida began to acquire much of the island's property, now known as Honeymoon Island State Park. At the southern end of the park, one can take the Caladesi Island Ferry to visit this neighboring island. In 1985, Hurricane Elena swept through this area and made another change in the island's topography. A huge sand deposit sealed off the entrance to Dunedin Pass, thereby connecting Clearwater Beach to Caladesi Island. From the north end of Clearwater Beach, one may walk to Caladesi Island on mostly dry beach sand at low tide. The walk is approximately 2.2 miles long, plus another two miles or more to reach the ranger station and concession stand in the island's center. It is a beautiful, but long, walk.

Three miles offshore from Tarpon Springs is the Anclote Key State Preserve, accessible only by private boat. I visited this island often with my parents, and they occasionally camped overnight on the island. This beautiful palm tree–lined beach is four miles long, its waters seen in several amazing shades of blue and green. The island is a paradise for shell collectors. Although no longer needed, the lighthouse on the island's southern tip has been restored.

All of the waters surrounding these islands are excellent fishing grounds. If the fish were busy elsewhere and not biting well, my father would pull up anchor and head for Hurricane Pass, a favorite pathway for fish to come and go from bay to gulf between Caladesi Island and Honeymoon Island. This was his never-to-fail fishing location. It was my father's best-kept secret, which he shared with only a few. This is why he could "sell" fish insurance.

Always during such outings, there would be an abundance of fish caught, fried, and enjoyed on a nearby island. And since these men were trust officers in a bank, they knew how important it was to earn and be worthy of the trust of others. In these outings, they were exposed to an unusual kind of trust experience—the guarantee of fish insurance by a very trustworthy fisherman.

After a number of such excursions with others, my father decided that I needed the same treatment. Off we went to a marina near Tarpon Springs. No side trips were made; we went directly to the pass between Caladesi Island and Honeymoon Island, well equipped with lots of bait. My father spent the entire time baiting my hook, and I pulled in fish after fish. The fish dinner that night was delicious.

I treasure this indelible memory of a father who wanted me to have the joy of a perfect day at his best-kept secret fishing hole, baiting my hook, just being together, Father and Daughter.

AFTERNOON SIESTA ON ANCLOTE KEY

A NARROW UNDERWATER ESCAPE

A pleasant day's fishing excursion in the abundant waters of lower Tampa Bay almost ended in disaster for two people I knew well—my parents.

After trolling the waters in vain for several hours, my father was ready to head home empty-handed when his fishing line went taut! Whatever had snapped up the bait was big and strong, and it required a patient and careful play of the line to bring the creature within reach. At last it broke the surface of the water—a shark! My experienced fisherman father decided to harvest his dangerous catch. His plan was to lean over the back of the boat, slowly pull in the feisty fish, and take him home to admire. As he leaned over the outboard motor, suddenly it flipped forward and propelled my father up into the air as if he were being shot out of a cannon. Then down, down he went headfirst into the murky bay waters to join a very irritated and disagreeable shark.

My father finally came to the surface, still wearing hat and sunglasses. He urgently called to my mother to throw him a life preserver since he needed to remove himself as soon as possible from the water before the jaws of the shark could find a place to attack. However, Mother was unable to respond to his call for help in a timely manner. My father reported that she did appear genuinely concerned, but she was so occupied doing a distraught "dance" in the boat that he had to swim over to the boat and crawl in all by himself. By that time, he was bleeding, so the shark had left its mark, but my father escaped with all limbs intact and required no stitches.

Dad took the shark home and buried it under an oak tree in the front yard, so he could "keep an eye on it."

HOW TO RETIRE GRACEFULLY

 e said goodbye to our bay cottage and boat when Dad's declining health made this decision necessary. After selling the cottage to a retiring couple that had just moved to Florida, he decided to bless them with the bonus of our boat, free of charge. This made our northern friends exceedingly happy, and my father walked away from his beloved cottage with a smile on his face and the joy of passing on his gift of happiness to others.

Never completely out of options, Dad still found ways to enjoy life. When he could no longer travel the waterways close to home, he began reading about the adventures of Captain James Cook, eighteenth-century sailor, surveyor, cartographer, explorer, and world traveler. My father sailed the seven seas with Captain Cook through the pages of Cook's journals and other books about his life. Together, they traveled to Tahiti, Brazil, the Canary Islands, New Zealand, Australia, Indonesia, and Africa, then back home to Great Britain, where they prepared for another exciting voyage.

There were still adventures to be enjoyed on a smaller scale nearby. Dad would say to Mother, "Dot, let's get some cold drinks and drive out to the boat-launching area on Davis Causeway." There, they would sit on the seawall, sipping their colas, and watch other people struggle with their boat-launching problems. They were often rewarded with some amusing entertainment. They reported that one man pushed off his friends' boat into the water, and then he yelled, "Wait a minute, I forgot to get in!"

The last excursion I had with my father took place on the St. Petersburg side of Gandy Bridge, where there are a few tiny islands close to the adjoining causeway. At low tide, we waded across a narrow channel and then walked through one of the islands to the other side where, hidden from the causeway and surrounded by palm trees, we could imagine being far away on a tropical island. We looked out over the bay where sailboats cruised the waters. There were enough shells to make me happy, a few fiddler crabs scuttling about, the overhead conversation of terns and seagulls, and the gentle lapping of the water against the shore. We leaned against some palm trees, got comfortable, and let the island bestow its usual magic touch upon us. We both knew there probably would not be another such adventure granted to us, so we savored each moment of this, our last island visit, together.

My father's last gift to me was his blessing, one that I will treasure forever. It came in the form of a bottle of rare wine with its vintage year, the same as my birth year, imprinted in gold numerals. As he placed the gift in my hands he said, "This was the best year of my life. Whenever you have a special event you want to celebrate, have a sip of this wine and remember how much you were loved." The wine is long gone, but the bottle remains in my possession together with the cherished memory of a father who gave me everything a daughter could ever desire from her father.

SAND IN YOUR SHOES

Do you long to travel south
When the thermostat dips low
And clouds drop their blankets
Of frost and icy snow?
Do you then dream of Florida
And wish that you were there,
To swim in warm Gulf waters
And smell the salty air,

Pick oranges and grapefruit right off a tree,
Fish for grouper in the deep blue sea,
Watch coastal sunsets on a carpet of sand,
Beachcomb for shells on subtropical islands?
To make these dreams come true
And escape those winter blues,
Just take some Florida beach sand
And sprinkle it into your shoes.

Soon you will ask yourself,
"Why wait any longer?"
Your desire to return to Florida
Will suddenly become much stronger!
It has worked for others.
It will work for you.
The Sunshine State is waiting,
Waiting just for you!

CONTENTMENT

 t was summertime, June, my favorite month of the year. I was on my way back home to Georgia after spending a relaxing week enjoying the Gulf beaches and all that Florida has to offer. Approaching the Florida/Georgia state line on I-75, I felt a wistful tug as I left my beloved home state. Then a Bible verse came to mind, the one about being content in whatever "state" you are in. I had just spent some time in St. Petersburg with one of my mentors, whose specialty was American calligraphy. I began planning how I would illustrate that verse, partly as a message to myself.

Life is an adventure, and there are joys to be found wherever you are. Each decade of our lives can be an interesting new chapter as we build on the ones that have gone before.

In my adoptive state of Georgia, gardening became one of my primary interests, and many happy hours were spent playing in the dirt. I became a Lifetime Master Gardener through the Georgia Extension Service. Studies in the art department at Georgia State University and my discovery of calligraphy brought new joys my way. I started my own calligraphy business and taught in various art schools in the Atlanta area. My love of beachcombing came in handy and just took another turn in the road. I began to search for hidden treasures in thrift stores, in forests as I gathered up pinecones to make wreaths, and along highways and byways, looking for unusual rocks to line our garden beds. My husband and I became "rock-out scientists" as we performed engineering feats to extricate unusually large rocks from their hiding places. We made no excuses for our love of puns.

My years in Florida are like a beautiful dream spent in a subtropical paradise. I hope my shared memories of yesteryear in Florida will bring joy to my readers. But life moves along, and there is always something "more" around the corner just as beautiful in its own way, if you look for it. I tried many avenues as I searched for my "place" in life, for that elusive place called *home*. In the search, I finally found it, not in a place, but in a personal relationship with Jesus Christ. During a point in my life when I needed a new purpose for living, the Lord gave me a special gift. I began to see God's creation through eyes of wonder and then capture what I saw with words and pictures. Albert Einstein said, "There are two ways to live your life. One is as though nothing is a miracle. The other is as though everything is a miracle."

There is beauty everywhere, just waiting for us to slow down and notice. Contentment can be ours, no matter what "state" we are in, when we are connected to the Lord of Life.

Mary Grable Renshaw

GEORGIA or FLORIDA NEW YORK IN JUNE or ALASKA

i HAVE LEARNED to
BE CONTENT
iN WHATEVER STATE i AM
i CAN DO ALL THINGS
THROUGH CHRIST
WHO
STRENGTHENS ME

Philippians 4:11,13

MOUNTAINTOP OR VALLEY LAKESIDE OR SEASHORE

MARRIED OR SINGLE RICH OR POOR SICK OR HEALTHY

RAIN or SHINE YOUNG or OLD RETIRED or WORKER

Mary Renshaw, Scribe

Contentment
Colored-Pencil Illustration

RECIPES

COQUINA CHOWDER

1 kettle coquinas (6 quarts)

1 medium onion, chopped and rinsed several times

1 tablespoon butter

Water to cover

2 cups milk or half-and-half

3 stalks celery, thinly sliced

½ teaspoon salt, or to taste

3 medium potatoes, diced

¼ teaspoon pepper or to taste

Cover coquinas with water; boil until shells open and broth is milky looking. Drain juice off through cheesecloth or fine sieve so only broth comes through. Place broth in saucepan with celery, potatoes, onion, and butter. Cook until potatoes are tender. Stir in milk and seasonings; heat thoroughly. Serves 6 to 8.

Coquinas are small, native periwinkle clams in rainbow colors that can be collected in a sieve at ebb tide on Florida beaches.

GULFCOAST BAY SCALLOPS

4 tablespoons butter

1 pound small bay scallops

2 or 3 tablespoons lemon juice

Salt and pepper to taste

Mix butter and lemon juice in heavy skillet. Add scallops; place in 400-degree oven. Shake occasionally; bake until brown, tender, and "glazed" (about 5 to 7 minutes). Sprinkle with salt and freshly ground pepper. Serves 3 to 4.

SPANISH BEAN SOUP

½ pound dried garbanzo beans

1 onion

1 tablespoon salt

2 ounces butter or oil

1 ham bone

1 pound potatoes

2 quarts water

Pinch of toasted saffron

Pinch of paprika

1 chorizo (Spanish sausage)

Salt to taste

1 bay leaf

Soak garbanzos overnight with a tablespoon of salt in sufficient water (at least 3 inches above beans). When ready to cook, drain the salted water from the beans and place them with the ham bone in the 2 quarts of water. Cook for 45 minutes over slow fire. Fry the onion in butter or oil. Add to the beans. Now, add peeled and cubed potatoes, saffron, and salt to taste. When potatoes are done remove from fire and add chorizo sausage cut in thin slices. Remove bay leaf. Serves 4.

Soup can be served together with crisp Cuban bread and a salad.

FLAN DE LECHE ACARAMELADO
SPANISH CARAMEL CUSTARD

1 pint milk	12 tablespoons sugar
¼ teaspoon salt	1 teaspoon vanilla
6 whole eggs	

Scald milk with the salt. In a suitable mixing bowl, beat eggs with 6 tablespoons of sugar and vanilla until light and foamy. Add scalded milk to egg mixture, stirring constantly. Set aside.

In a small iron skillet, sprinkle 6 tablespoons of sugar. Place skillet over low heat and cook until a foamy golden caramel is obtained (be careful not to burn the sugar). Immediately pour into a 1½ quart casserole and quickly coat the bottom of the casserole by rotating and tilting it until it is completely coated. Allow to set for only a few seconds.

Pour egg mixture into casserole. Place casserole in shallow pan with hot water (baño maría). Set oven at 275 degrees and place pan in center of oven. Cook for approximately one hour, or until custard is set.

Test for doneness by inserting a knife in the center of the custard. When it comes out clean, the custard is done. When the custard has a golden-yellow crust, this is an indication that it is ready to be removed from the oven. Do not allow water to boil in the baño maría.

Cool, cover, and refrigerate. Serve chilled. Yields 6 servings.

The custard can be removed from the casserole by running a knife around the edge, shaking lightly, and inverting onto a serving dish. The caramel sauce will drip down the side of the casserole and form a delicious covering over the custard. Serve in sherbet cups or dessert saucers. Add a cookie on the side if desired.

For individual custards, divide the caramel quickly among 6 custard cups; allow to set, then pour egg mixture into each cup and cook at 350 degrees for 30 minutes in a pan with water.

For a perfect outcome, make sure that you beat the eggs sufficiently (count slowly to 25). Don't let the water boil in the baño maría (add a little water to the pan to avoid this if necessary), and do not let the custard remain in the oven too long. If the crust is brown, it has been overcooked.

ENJOY!

ABOUT THE AUTHOR

Author Mary Grable Renshaw left her beloved home state of Florida in her midtwenties to take up residence in the captivating metropolis of Atlanta, Georgia.

When she met Dr. Parke Renshaw, then a college professor and former missionary for the United Methodist Church in Brazil, it set into motion a life-changing adventure for them both. Parke was on his way back to Brazil to work with the Methodist University of Piracicaba in the State of São Paulo. He asked Mary to accompany him. She said yes, and the two were married in 1978. The move required Mary to leave behind everything that had been her life. Such abrupt changes were not easy; however, the rewards were more than she could have imagined.

Parke and Mary lived for four years in Brazil. After Mary learned Portuguese, she used her training as an artist to teach art history in the university. Their amazing adventures have been recounted in Mary's first book, entitled *Look at the Moon*, published in 2018.

Upon their return to the United States, Parke and Mary moved to Decatur, Georgia, in the Atlanta metro area. She and her husband created a garden ambiance at their home they named "Renshaw Park." Parke passed away in 2010 before Mary's book was published.

Mary still lives in Decatur and is the founder of her own business, Noteworthy Cards and Capital Letters. She is a member of the Atlanta Friends of the Alphabet, a calligraphy guild, and The Scribblers, a Christian writers' group.

Mary's love for her home state of Florida and the memories that were created there become more beautiful with every passing day.

**OTHER BOOKS BY
MARY GRABLE RENSHAW**

Look at the Moon

CONTRIBUTOR

Pens in the Piedmont